Fiddle Time Scales

Musicianship and technique through scales

Kathy and David Blackwell

MUSIC DEPARTMENT

OXFORD

UNIVERSITY PRESS

OXFORD
UNIVERSITY PRESS

Great Clarendon Street, Oxford OX2 6DP, England

Oxford University Press is a department of the University of Oxford.
It furthers the University's aim of excellence in research, scholarship,
and education by publishing worldwide

Oxford is a registered trade mark of Oxford University Press
in the UK and in certain other countries

ISBN 978–0–19–338641–9

Music and text origination by
Barnes Music Engraving Ltd., East Sussex
Printed in Great Britain on acid-free paper by
Halstan & Co. Ltd., Amersham, Bucks.

Authors' note
All pieces are original compositions unless stated otherwise.

With grateful thanks to Liz Beynon and Mark Levy
for their help with this book.

Contents

Getting to know your scales:

• Play them:

1. With even notes and separate bows:

2. Slurred two notes to a bow:

• Play them with a long note on the key note or tonic:

• learn the key signature for each key, know the letter names, and mark the semitones like this: ⌞⌟ (see p. 4)

• play a tune you know well in that key by ear

• use the notes of the scale and arpeggio to make up your own compositions

• play with different kinds of bow strokes: legato, martelé, spiccato, broken slurs, etc.

• play with different dynamics and tempos—what's your top speed (scales p.h.)?

G major, 2 octaves

Scale

Most scales are made up of patterns of tones and semitones. The major scale uses this pattern:
    Tone, tone, semitone, tone, tone, tone, semitone
like this:

Mark the semitones like this in the scales and pieces as you work through the book.

Arpeggio

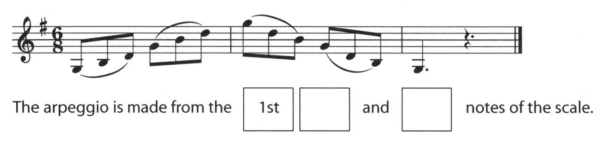

The arpeggio is made from the [1st] [ ] and [ ] notes of the scale.

Keep fit

* To add a second part, play the descending scale of G major in semibreves (whole notes). Play the upper octave for the second half.

The Arrival of the Queen of Sheba

G. F. Handel

A major, 2 octaves

Scale

Arpeggio

Question and answer

'What instrument do you play?' 'I play the violin.'
A lot of tunes are made from questions and answers—a short musical phrase or 'question' is answered by a balancing phrase.

Here's a well-known tune built in this way:

The notes and note values are similar between the question and answer—one flows from the other. If someone asks 'What instrument do you play?', you wouldn't answer with 'I like pizza and chips'!

The last note of the answer makes it sound finished or unfinished. Experiment with different notes in your answers to these questions:

Out of the question

Play questions and answers in this duet, returning to the chorus after each verse. Make up and write down a question and answer of your own in the 3rd verse. Add your own dynamics!

Bb major, 2 octaves

Scale

Scale warm ups

Play the scale with this bowing pattern:

etc.

Try this for fit fingers:

* May also be played as a two-part round, entering at *

Arpeggio

Arpeggio warm up

Play this fanfare for two.

Composition

Here's the start of a tune in Bb major. Use the notes from the scale to complete it. Add dynamics and a title.

Confident

Mock Baroque

Dotted rhythm warm up

E major, 1 octave

Scale

Mark the semitones with ⌐_⌐

Arpeggio

Play the scale of E major with hooked bowing:

etc.

Hook or by crook

Banuwa

African

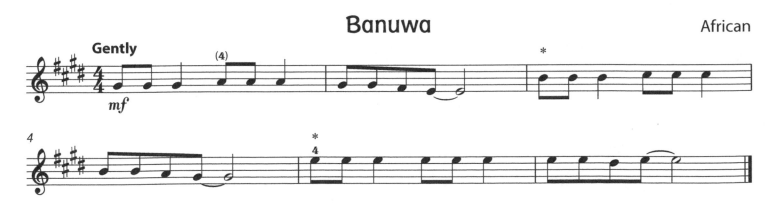

* Play as a three-part round, entering at *

E minor, 1 octave

Harmonic

Melodic

Play these scales using this bowing pattern:

etc.　　　* Whole Bow

Arpeggio

In your stride

Composition

Here is the start of a tune in E minor. Use the notes from the harmonic or melodic scale to finish it off. Try using different techniques, like tremolo bowing, glissandi, or pizzicato, to add atmosphere to your piece. Give it a title and add dynamics too.

E♭ major, 1 octave

Scale

Arpeggio

Scale game for 2 players

Player 1 invents a different 1 bar rhythm for each degree of the scale, player 2 copies.
Swap around for the descending scale.

For example:

Variations
Also try this game with different bow-strokes (tremolo, spiccato, etc.), or arco/pizz., or different
dynamics for each bar, etc.

You can try this in any key!

Tallis's canon

Thomas Tallis

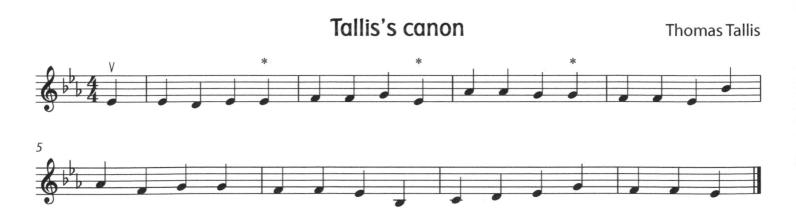

* Play as a canon or round, entering at *

A♭ major, 1 octave

Scale

Arpeggio

Stop—start

Warm up

As always, use the rests to get your fingers ready for the next pattern; don't play in the rests!

13

D major, 2 octaves

Scale

(stay in 3rd position)

Play the scale with spiccato bowing, keeping to the middle/lower half of the bow:

etc.

Arpeggio

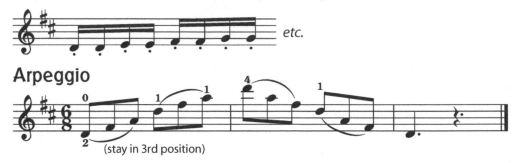

(stay in 3rd position)

Spic and span

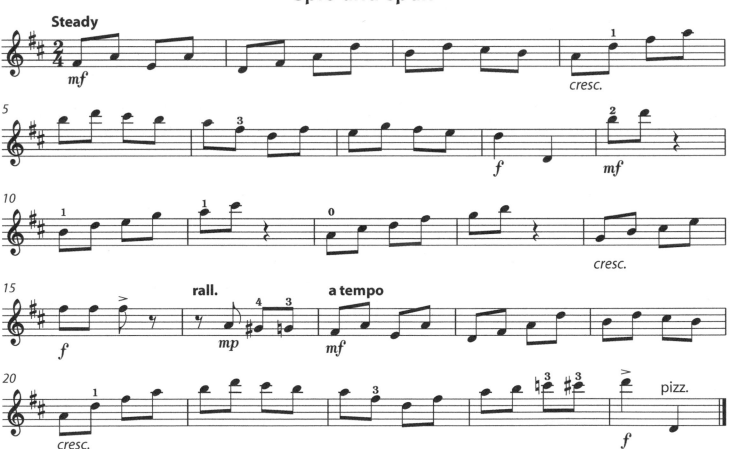

Variation: play with 2 semiquavers to each note and spiccato bowing.

Scale game for 2 players

Use only the notes of the D major scale. Player 1 plays open D and adds on one more note of their choice. Player 2 copies these two notes and adds on one more note. Player 1 copies in turn, again adding a further note. And so on. Game over when someone forgets! For example:

Allegro in D

E. P. Chédeville

(stay in 3rd position)

Esprit Philippe Chédeville was a French musician and instrument-maker of the 18th century.

D minor, 2 octaves

Harmonic

2 (stay in 3rd position)

Melodic

Arpeggio

Try the scales and arpeggio with martelé bowing. 'Martelé' is French for 'hammered' and indicates a strong staccato bow stroke, usually played in the upper half of the bow.

Snake bite

Strong

f martelé

mf

(stay in 3rd position until *)

f

mf

*

Which version of the minor scale is used in this piece? ....

Tango

Warm ups

Play these scales in these rhythms:

Wake up! and do the tan-go, wake up! and do the tan-go,

Have a si - es - ta, have a si - es - ta,

Be sure to make a difference between these rhythms. Keep the triplet *lazy*.

Now try the twiddly bit!

A minor, 2 octaves

Harmonic

Harmonic minor warm up

Melodic

Melodic minor warm up

Arpeggio

Composition

Composers sometimes build pieces from a short theme or tune which is then varied in different ways. For example, they might vary the rhythm or the shape of the melody, or use different bowing styles or dynamics. Try writing your own variations on this short theme in A minor.

Theme

5 **Variation 1**

9 **Variation 2**

Theme and variations

Chromatics, 1 octave

on D

Use the same finger pattern to play the chromatic scales starting on the G and A strings.

Make a very definite movement with 1st and 2nd fingers when they move from low to high position.

Try playing with slurred bowing, either 4 or 6 notes to a bow. It can help if you say this while you play:

Down for 4 notes, up for 4 notes, etc.   Down-bow for 6 notes and up-bow for 6 notes and, etc.

Chromatic warm ups

Play this pattern, marking T for tone or S for semitone in the boxes:

Write out and play the same pattern starting on the A string.

Practise moving the 1st finger with this warm up:

Now try on the other strings.

Circus act

Dominant 7ths, 1 octave

In the key of G

In the key of D

In the key of C

Write out the notes for the dominant 7th in the key of C. The first note is given.

Which finger plays in both high and low position? ....

Why is it called the dominant 7th? The starting note is the 5th note of the scale, also called the **dominant**. The chord or arpeggio shape based on this note uses the 3rd, 5th, and **7th** degrees from the dominant.

Divide the notes between two players like this. Play at the same time to hear the dominant 7th as a chord (or play on a piano).

Player 1

D7   A7   G7

Player 2

Seventh heaven

Sunny

f

5   *Fine*

9

mf

13   *rall.*   *D.C. al Fine*

cresc.

✗ Tap your violin with your left hand, or stamp your foot.

Which bar contains all the notes of the dominant 7th: in G ....? in D ....? in C ....?

Pentatonics, 2 octaves

Major pentatonic on D

Pentatonic scales are scales with five notes. They are found in music from all round the world, for example China, Japan, Latin America, and Africa, and in some European folk music, especially from Scotland and Ireland.

Play by ear

Here is the start of two well-known major pentatonic tunes; see if you can continue them by ear:

'Auld Lang Syne'   'Amazing grace'

You've already played another major pentatonic tune in this book—did you spot it?

Composition

Compose your own major pentatonic tune using this rhythm:

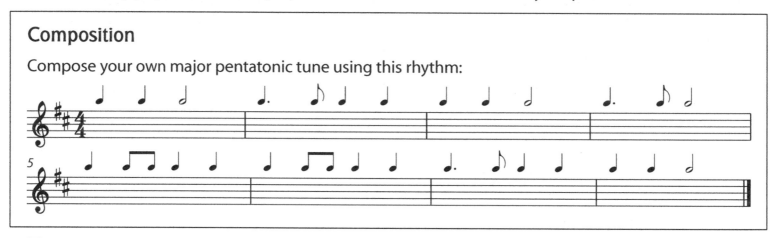

Warm up

On Loch Lubnaig

The chord symbols are for keyboard or guitar accompaniment.

Flat 3 pentatonic on D

In the flat 3 pentatonic the 3rd note is lowered, giving the scale a minor feel. The F♮–B♮ interval creates a special colour, characteristically found in the blues and Eastern European folk music.

Flat tyre warm up

Keep your thumb opposite first finger when you move position.

Flat tyre blues

Gypsy warm ups

Also play 2 quavers and 4 semiquavers to each note.

Gypsy wedding

G minor, 2 octaves

Harmonic

Melodic

Mark the semitones with ⌐_⌐ in these two scales—be careful!

Arpeggio

Spanish dance

Trad.

Menuet

Christian Petzold

from *The Anna Magdalena Bach Book* (1725)

Modes, 2 octaves

Dorian on D

Modes are types of scales found in many different kinds of music, for example Western music of the Middle Ages (e.g. plainsong), folk music from many countries, and in some forms of jazz. There are a number of different types, each with their own pattern of tones and semitones and character.

Bowing warm up

Play one octave of the mode in this rhythm. Use almost as much bow for the crotchets as you do for the minims, using a quick and gentle up-bow stroke.

Scarborough Fair

English Trad.

Play with guitar or keyboard accompaniment and a drum playing this rhythm: ♩. ♪♩

Mixolydian on D

Which note in the Mixolydian mode is different from the Dorian? ....

The F♯ and C♮ in the Mixolydian mode given it its special flavour. Be sure to move 2nd finger backwards and forwards in 'Old Joe Clark' like this:

Old Joe Clark

Trad. American fiddle tune

Swap parts on the repeats.
Try playing 'Old Joe Clark' (from bar 4) starting on the open E string (Mixolydian on A).

F major, 1 octave

Scale

Arpeggio

This scale and arpeggio can be played in either 1st or 2nd position. The 2nd position fingering is given in brackets.

2nd position warm up

Play with different bow strokes:
Detaché: lower half of the bow for the first 2 bars, then upper half of the bow for the second 2 bars.
Legato: slurring 4 quavers to a bow and using whole bows.
Dotted rhythm: ♩. ♪
Spiccato: playing semiquavers instead of quavers and minims.

Play by ear

Play 'Happy Birthday' in F major.
1. In 1st position starting on 3rd finger on the G string (C);
2. In 2nd position starting on 1st finger on the A string (C an octave higher).

Question and answer

Give answers to these questions in F major.

Sea shanty

Trad.

Warm up

Round the Bay of Mexico

Trad.

Swap parts on the repeat.

C major, 1 octave

Scale

Arpeggio

Play by ear

1. Here's the start of a well-known tune in C major. See if you can play it by ear in 2nd position.

'Oh when the saints'

2. Play the African round 'Banuwa' on p. 10 in the key of C major in 2nd position. Here's the first bar:

Autumn
from *The Four Seasons*

Antonio Vivaldi

Allegro

(stay in 2nd position)

Jig warm up

Three Scottish Jigs
Green holm

Play these jigs as a set, one after the other. The middle jig could be played a little slower as a contrast; it uses the Dorian mode on A.

Blues scale, 1 octave

on D

(stay in 2nd position)

Use the same finger pattern to play the blues scale starting on the open G or open A string.

The blues scale contains the main notes you need to play the blues, especially the flattened 3rd, 5th, and 7th, the so-called 'blue' notes.

Composition

Try making up your own blues tune using this rhythm:

Blues for Scrapper

'Scrapper' Blackwell was an American blues guitarist in the 1930s (no relation!).